Naturally Healthy Living
With Diatomaceous Earth

*You, your home, and your pets can be healthier
using Mother Earth's Best Kept Secret!*

L. A. Nicholas, Ph. D.

DISCLAIMER

The information contained in this book is for information purposes only. All information is correct to the best of the author's knowledge, but nothing contained herein should be taken as medical advice. Readers should use their own good judgment in using this information, and take note of all warnings mentioned. In particular, consult a doctor or veterinarian if you believe you or your pet has any medical condition that might be treated with diatomaceous earth. The author of this book cannot be held responsible for the use or misuse of the information given.

CONTENTS

INTRODUCTION

D o you want a "greener" home? Are you tired of buying expensive, toxic cleaners? Do you wish there was a cheap, safe, and effective way to rid your home of bed bugs and other six-legged pests? Do the flea control products you buy make your pets sicker than they do the fleas? Do you need a safe, gentle product to worm your pets and keep them free from parasites? Do you prefer natural remedies to potentially dangerous pharmaceutical treatments? If you answered yes to any of these questions, this book was written for you.

Perhaps you are like me, wanting to get back to nature in finding ways to keep yourself and your home clean and healthy. I have for many years preferred to use natural products and simple home remedies, rather than relying on the toxic chemicals, expensive brand name potions, and dangerous pharmaceuticals that have become part of our modern way of life. Yet I am also a bit dubious when I read about "miracle" foods and substances; I'd like to believe in them, but I know that many of the claims can't be true, so I read carefully and weigh the evidence before I buy into some of the kooky claims that proliferate on the internet. (Remember when apricot pits were supposed to hold the key to curing cancer?)

When I first started learning about the many uses of diatomaceous earth, I was a bit skeptical, but as I began researching, learning about the physical properties of this substance, reading expert studies, etc. I became more convinced that many of the claims were reasonable (no, I don't believe it will cure cancer!). I've used it myself in most of the ways suggested in this booklet, and those I have not tried (for instance, using DE to get rid of bedbugs) are well-attested by hundreds of people who have tried them. So everything in this book is something I believe in and can recommend in good faith. I am not trying to convince you that diatomaceous earth is a "miracle cure" for anything, but I do think it is a very useful substance that should be particularly helpful to anyone who is interested in being thrifty, ecologically responsible, and healthy.

If you try any of the treatments in this little book and find success, please drop me a line and tell me about it. Just send me an email at writernicholas@gmail.com.

MOTHER EARTH'S BEST-KEPT SECRET?

Diatomaceous earth (DE) is a wonderful secret that Mother Earth kept for millions of years, until a German peasant digging a well in the nineteenth century discovered a deposit of what at first appeared to be limestone. Since that time, this abundantly available mineral has attracted lots of attention for industrial and agricultural uses, and in recent decades has also gained popularity for a variety of uses in and around the home, both for eliminating pests and for promoting health.

WHAT IS DIATOMACEOUS EARTH?

What is this wonderful substance? Diatomaceous earth is a white, chalky material formed from the fossilized remains of tiny, ancient one-celled algae organisms, called diatoms (diatomaceous means "full of diatoms"). Although similar organisms (living ones!) still fill our water sources today, contributing to the aquatic food chain, diatomaceous earth is composed of the remains of tiny creatures from millions of years ago in the Cenozoic era, when animal life was first developing on our planet. These microscopic creatures' bodies were encased in silica exoskeletons, and as the diatoms died they sank to the bottoms of the bodies of water in which they had lived. The silicate shells remained, creating a sediment, and over the eons this sediment became compacted and fossilized, eventually forming a white sedimentary rock. Now, in a number of locations around the country and around the world, this rock is quarried and crushed to powder to allow it to be used for a variety of purposes today.

There are two general sources of diatomaceous earth, marine deposits (from places where there once was salt water) and freshwater deposits, which provide food-grade DE. This latter sort is what we are interested in, as it is the only kind safe for mammals — i.e., you and your pets. Marine (non-food grade) DE has a crystalline structure that makes it unsafe to be inhaled or ingested, while freshwater DE lacks this jagged crystalline structure, making it safe for use in the home where pets and humans live. Keep this in mind — you should always make sure that you purchase and use "food grade" diatomaceous earth. Manufacturers will usually indicate prominently the quality of the product, so it is easy to make sure you are getting the kind you need.

Before looking at household uses of DE, it is worth knowing about some of general properties of this substance and its various uses outside the home.

If you open a bag or jar of diatomaceous earth, you will see a fine, whitish powder that looks and feels a lot like talcum powder or chalk dust. Although the powder feels soft to the touch, microscopic particle is actually quite hard. Diatomaceous earth is a form of amorphous silica (i.e., silica that does not have a crystalline structure), composed mostly of silicon, with trace amounts of iron, sodium, and magnesium. The honeycomb structure of the diatoms makes it very porous and therefore useful as a medium for filtration. In fact, one of its earliest uses after being discovered in the mid-1800's was in Alfred Nobel's earliest formulation of dynamite, because the porous DE could absorb nitroglycerin and render it less volatile. Because DE is inert (it does not react chemically with other substances), it was safer in dynamite production than some of the organic materials that Nobel experimented with, such as sawdust.

Diatomaceous earth also makes a good thermal barrier, so it is sometimes used in building fire-proof safes — and in cryogenics, to keep things very cold. The absorbent quality of DE also makes it useful for cleaning up chemical spills, and it is even used in facial masks to absorb body oils from the skin. Its absorbency also makes DE useful in agricultural storage of grains, as an anti-caking agent.

The porous character of the microscopic diatom shells make diatomaceous earth useful in filtering liquids, so today one of the most common industrial uses of DE is as a filtration medium. It is used in water filtration, both in swimming pools and in drinking water filtration, because it can trap bacteria and particles so tiny that they would pass through other kinds of filters, such as paper. DE filtration is also used in the beer- and wine-making industries. Be aware, however, that the kind of DE generally used for filtration is not safe for household or agricultural uses. Industrial grade DE has been subjected to high heat and chemicals that change its structure from an amorphous one to a crystalline one. Crystalline particles are very sharp and jagged, making them dangerous if inhaled in any quantity, so you should not use this kind of DE around your home.

Another useful property of diatomaceous earth is its gently abrasive quality — the silicon structure makes it hard, but the microscopic size of the diatoms gives it an extremely fine grit. For this reason, you will find some household metal polishes that contain DE, and it is also found in some toothpastes to remove plaque build-up.

USES IN & AROUND
THE HOME

As you can see, you have probably already experienced, indirectly, some of the benefits of diatomaceous earth, without even knowing it. Now, however, let's look at some of the ways DE can be useful in your daily life. (Keep in mind that here we'll be talking about freshwater, or "food grade" DE.) Let's start outside your home, in the garden, and see how DE can be of use there.

IN THE YARD AND GARDEN

One of the most common uses of diatomaceous earth in and around the home is as a pesticide. Incredibly, although it is very safe for pets and people, DE can be quite deadly to bugs. To understand how this can be true, we need to recall DE's abrasive and absorbent qualities. These combine to give most bugs a one-two knockout punch: the honey-combed hard silica structure of the diatom cuts through the outer covering of the insect, which exposes its moist innards, and the absorbency of the DE sucks the fluids right out of the bug. Just walking, crawling, or slithering across a surface coated with diatomaceous earth will kill most bugs within a few minutes: death by desiccation. DE is deadly not only to insects and spiders, but also to snails and slugs — these critters don't even have a hard surface to protect their moist flesh.

ON YOUR PLANTS

The usefulness of diatomaceous earth as a pesticide makes it very popular with organic gardeners: plants of all kinds can be dusted with DE instead of Sevin dust (or even more dangerous chemical pesticides). Food grade DE is not toxic to the plant or to people or pets who might want to eat the plant or its fruit, but if bugs try to dine on a DE-dusted plant, it will be their last meal. You can feel safe dusting your vegetable garden, your roses, your potted plants, or even your lawn with diatomaceous earth, knowing that you are not bringing toxic chemicals into your yard or garden. Just remember that inhaling a lot of dust (DE or any other kind) is not good for you or your pets, so if you are spreading large quantities of

DE you should wear a dust mask and goggles, and put the pets inside until the dust settles. Keep in mind, too, that rain or sprinkler systems may wash the DE off your plants, so you will need to reapply it afterward.

Don't worry if the DE gets into the soil, however. In fact, it may even be beneficial to your plants, because plants and their roots need silica to resist disease, and a small amount of the silica in diatomaceous earth is the soluble kind. This soluble silica becomes available for the plants when the DE gets wet, while the remaining insoluble silica remains porous and absorbent, and will therefore retain water, keeping the soil moist longer. For this reason, hydroponic gardeners often use diatomite (diatomaceous earth in the form of small rocks rather than powder) as a growing medium, and bonsai gardeners like to mix it in with their potting soil, peat, or other growth medium.

IN YOUR YARD

There may be other bugs you want to be rid of, besides those that attack your plants. What about ants? Sprinkle some DE around the top of an anthill, or anywhere that you know ants travel, and they'll soon be dead. (The fact that ants tend to play follow-the-leader means that where one ant has gone, the rest will soon go, too.) Any bugs that crawl into your house from outdoors can be, quite literally, stopped dead in their tracks if you sprinkle DE on the pavement, along cracks at the bottoms of walls, in the tracks of sliding doors, and other places where pests may try to get into your home. Crickets, flies, and millipedes are among the pests that can be eliminated with diatomaceous earth. If you have outdoor pets and have problems with fleas or ticks, you can protect your animals by dusting the lawn, as well as the pets' bedding, with DE. If you normally use flea & tick powder on your pets (the kind that you rub in to get it next to their skin), why not throw out your toxic chemical flea powder and start using diatomaceous earth instead? It won't hurt your pets anymore than talcum powder hurts you when you sprinkle it on yourself after a shower. Do you already use a "natural," non-toxic flea and tick powder product? Take a close look at the label — you may find that it says "diatomaceous earth."

INSIDE YOUR HOME

Now let's go indoors and see what we can do with diatomaceous earth there. First, here are a couple of ways diatomaceous earth can help you keep your home clean and fresh. The gently abrasive quality of DE makes it useful as a polish for hard surfaces — just make a paste with water and scour your porcelain sinks, cooking pots, or silver service without fear of scratching them. You can also sprinkle a little DE powder on your toothpaste before you brush your teeth for extra cleaning power — the gently-abrasive action will leave your teeth feeling smooth and plaque-free.

The absorbent quality of DE makes it effective as a household deodorizer — you can set an open container of DE in the back of your fridge or cupboard to keep them smelling fresh, instead of using baking soda. Diatomaceous earth will also deodorize your garbage cans — just sprinkle some in the bottom of the bin before putting in a new plastic liner — or your shoes. A layer of DE on top of your cat's litter, or mixed into it, will absorb moisture and inhibit odors.

If you find bugs that have managed to slither or crawl their way into your home, DE can help you get rid of them, just as it does in the garden. All sorts of creepy-crawlies like to cohabit with humans: silverfish, earwigs, weevils, cockroaches, crickets, spiders, bed bugs, and others. All of these can be killed with diatomaceous earth at no risk to you, your children, or your pets. When you buy your DE, you may want to pick up a small bulb duster or puffer that will allow you to put the DE just where you need it — for instance, along baseboards and window sills, in the backs of cupboards, and other places that bugs like to travel, but where you will be unlikely to track the dust out into the open. DE is as safe to use as a pesticide inside the four walls of your home as it is outside.

IN THE BEDROOM

One of the insect pests that has recently made a comeback inside people's homes and, even worse, in their beds, is the physically tiny yet psychologically devastating bedbug. If you've ever suffered, or known anyone who suffered, a bedbug infestation, you know that the process of eliminating a home of this insidious pest can be long and nerve-wracking. Residents whose homes are infested with bedbugs are usually advised to seal up all possible points of entry with caulking (difficult to do because these pests are tiny and can crawl through crevices you can't even see), clean and disinfect all bedding and other soft goods, isolate beds from other furniture, and have their homes professionally treated with toxic chemicals. But even if these measures succeed in getting rid of the pests, at what cost? The lingering effects of the pesticidal poisons may continue to present a risk to human and animal inhabitants.

Many people seeking a safe and effective pesticide that can be used to eliminate bedbugs have turned to diatomaceous earth, with excellent results. DE works on bedbugs just as it works on the fleas, ants, and other bugs already discussed, but it must be properly used, in combination with other prudent measures. Ideally, you want to keep them out of the bed, rather than killing them once they get there, since it is very difficult to eradicate these pests from mattresses or pillows once these have been infested. You should move the bed away from walls, draperies, etc., so that the pests can't jump or fall onto it. However, unless you know how to make your bed float in midair, even if you move it away from walls, etc., bedbugs will still be able to get to it from the floor, so that is the place to attack them with DE. One way to do this is to sprinkle a layer of DE all over the floor under and immediately around the bed. If you are concerned that this will be too messy, you can purchase bedbug trays, round plastic trays with a trough around them: place each foot of the bed in the center of a tray and fill the trough with diatomaceous earth. (You can easily improvise such trays, using small paper plates.)When the bedbug treks through the DE powder to crawl up the leg of the bed, it will be killed just as any other bug would be, and you soon may be able to enjoy a good night's sleep without fear of becoming a bedbug's midnight snack.

IN THE KITCHEN

While we are on the subject of many-legged uninvited guests in your home, let's head out to the kitchen and poke around in the pantry. If you have problems with weevils or other pests getting into stored dry foods such as rice, beans, or flour, you can safely mix a little DE powder in with the food. If you already have such food items in airtight containers, just spoon in a little of the powder, close the container's lid tightly, and shake it until the DE is evenly dispersed. Not only will this stop bugs from turning your rice or bean canister into a bug diner, but it will also keep the food dry and stop it from caking. Don't worry, diatomaceous earth is virtually tasteless and completely edible — you did buy "food grade," didn't you? — so you will not even notice the presence of DE powder when you cook your beans, rice, or whatever.

This brings us to a question that may have been hovering in the back of your mind: why would "diatomaceous earth" (isn't earth dirt?) come in "food grade" (who would want to eat dirt?)? Well, I hope you realize by now that DE is not "dirt." In fact, it looks like cornstarch or flour and has no noticeable taste. But the "food grade" label is not necessarily intended to encourage people to eat it. DE is much more often consumed by animals than humans — added to the feed of livestock to keep cattle, horses, and other barnyard animals healthy and their food free of insects. It is even approved by the United States Department of

Agriculture and the Food and Drug Administration for such uses. Although not everything that is healthy for an animal to eat is equally safe for humans, food grade diatomaceous earth is generally regarded as safe for all mammals, and that includes us "featherless bipeds." So human consumption of diatomaceous earth is perfectly safe.

HEALTH BENEFITS

Would anyone really want to eat diatomaceous earth? If so, why? In fact, many people do consume a little DE each day for their health, and a wide variety of benefits are claimed by enthusiastic DE users, some of them quite reasonable and others a bit more far-fetched. Let's begin by looking at the most reasonable claims, and leave some of the others until later. It seems reasonable to expect health benefits in humans who consume DE similar to those produced in animals when they are fed DE by their human handlers, and in fact this seems to be the case. One of the reasons farms and breeders add DE to their animals' food is to prevent and/or rid the animals of parasitic infections, including tapeworms, heart worms, lung worms, and the many other kinds of parasites that can attack domesticated animals. Diatomaceous earth has an excellent track record in treating animals for parasites (it kills them as effectively as it kills insects), and it is cheap as well as effective, with no known side-effects, making it easy to see why it is a common additive to the feed of cattle, horses, pigs, chickens, and other farm animals.

PET HEALTH

You can keep your dog or cat free of parasites in much the way that farms, stables, and kennels do with their animals: by mixing a little DE in with your pet's food each day. A teaspoonful or two is enough for a grown cat or a small dog; larger pets should get a bit more, proportionate to body weight (no more than two or three tablespoons a day for a large dog). If you store dry pet food in plastic bins, you can add a quantity of DE and shake the container to disperse it, much as you would do with a food container in your pantry.

Since parasites lay eggs inside the host's body and it may take weeks for all the eggs to hatch, if you are treating your pet with DE you should keep it up daily for at least 90 days to make sure that parasites from any eggs that hatch will continue to be eliminated. Many pet owners who give their animals DE, however, simply make it a daily supplement taken over the long term, since pets are constantly exposing themselves to re-infestation in their daily jaunts into the back yard.

YOUR HEALTH

At this point you may be thinking, "Okay, animals get into all sorts of nasty things, so it's easy to see why they need to be protected from worms and other parasites. But ... humans? I don't drink out of dirty puddles or eat unwashed vegetables or undercooked pork, so I'll never pick up a parasite." Perhaps you won't, but getting parasites is much easier and more common than you may think, and not only in third-world countries with poor public sanitation.

The fact is that many people are infested with parasites without realizing it; even if they notice that they are feeling lousy and have their family physician test them for parasites, the test may return a false negative result, because medical tests screen for only 40 or 50 of the more than 1,000 types of parasites that can attack the human body. So you are more likely to be unknowingly infected than you may think.

What are the effects of having parasites living inside your body, in your gut, lungs, liver, or other internal organs? Many of them are not obvious, which is why a person may be infested without realizing it — the basic law of survival requires that parasites seem innocuous or go undetected, so the host will tolerate them. (Think about it — if you discovered that you had parasites in your body, wouldn't your immediate response be to scream, "Yuck, get it out of me!" and then do everything in your power to do so?) The wide variety of symptoms that may indicate the effects of an undetected parasite includes chronic pain, lethargy, anal itching, aching joints, bloating, numbness, brain fog, and a host of others. Some of these symptoms might mistakenly be attributed to other causes or to something as vague as "getting older" or being "run down." While I do not encourage you to engage in self-diagnosis in place of competent medical care (if you are experiencing severe or persistent symptoms, get thee to a doctor!), you may find it worth your while to try taking diatomaceous earth for a couple of weeks to see if it relieves your symptoms. In itself, DE is safe and you may also find it effective, as many other people have done.

Even those who are not afflicted with parasites, however, may experience health benefits from taking a tablespoon of DE every day, in a glass of juice or water, sprinkled on their breakfast cereal, or mixed in with yogurt or a breakfast smoothie. If you surf the Internet for DE testimonials, you will find that many people report that within a couple of weeks they notice a greater sense of energy, more regular bowel movements, clearer skin, lower blood pressure, and stronger, healthier hair and nails. Some people say their achy joints quit aching since they've been taking diatomaceous earth every day; others claim they lost weight after beginning to take DE every day — without altering their diet or habits in any other way. (The most outrageous claim I've even seen is that it cures cancer, but I would take that one with a grain – or a whole box – of salt.)

Although there have been no scientific studies to evaluate most of these claims, there may be a reasonable explanation for many of these alleged health benefits (and perhaps some day the scientific and medical communities will get around to "proving" what many DE users say they already know). One reason diatomaceous earth makes some people feel better or look healthier may have to do with the fact that DE is made up mostly of silica (80% or more, some of it soluble), an element that the body needs to maintain good health. Silica helps build collagen in the joints, blood vessels, and connective tissues, as well as healthy skin, hair, and nails, so perhaps it should not be surprising that people who begin taking a daily dose of silica (DE) report that their knee pain disappears, their skin clears up, their nails are healthier and stronger, their hair becomes glossier, etc. Our modern diets are often made up of highly refined foods whose natural silica content is lost in the process of refinement, so supplemental silica can help maintain the level of health that nature ought to provide.

Alleviation of other symptoms reported by DE users may be attributed to the detoxifying effects of diatomaceous earth. Because of their honeycombed shape, the microscopic diatoms can trap toxins in your digestive tract, and even gently scrub the inside of your colon as they pass through. Silica is also known to fight plaque buildup on artery walls, which can help maintain a healthy cardio-vascular system and keep blood cholesterol and pressure low. There is scientific evidence showing that DE binds heavy metals and other environmental toxins and removes them from the body, which would explain why DE users report that their digestion, mental clarity, and immune function improve.

CAUTIONS

If you decide to start taking DE as a daily supplement, please make sure that you increase your fluid intake to offset the absorptive power of the powder. Also, be aware that the first day or two you may temporarily feel worse as your body experiences a "healing crisis" while it detoxifies and your immune system recovers from its stupor. But even if you are very excited and eager to begin experiencing the health benefits of DE, you should not overdo it or jump in too quickly. It is wise to start with just half a teaspoonful each day, and slowly increase until you are taking about a tablespoonful (more or less depending on your size — aim for about half a tablespoonful per 100 pounds of body weight). Keep this in mind, too, if you decide to add DE to your pets' diets: don't give them too much, and make sure they have plenty of fresh water.

Remember not to confuse food grade diatomaceous earth (safe for humans and animals) with industrial grade, marine, swimming pool, or calcined DE, which are NOT SAFE for humans or animals. Food grade diatomaceous earth can be purchased in garden centers, agricultural supply houses, and health food stores, but if you can't find it in your area it is widely available through online retailers. Prices vary, so shop around. I know of one excellent brand available in a two-pound bag for less than ten dollars (plus shipping), but some retailers will ask twice that amount. Compare products, read customer reviews, and pick the source that seems best to you.

Finally, in using DE, as in all things, exercise caution and good sense in evaluating extravagant claims. Consult your doctor if you have a medical condition that might be affected by DE. In particular, anyone suffering from ailments such as bleeding ulcers, colitis, leaky gut syndrome, or advanced lupus should be sure to check with their doctor before taking DE internally, as it may make these conditions worse.

SUMMARY

What is it?

Food Grade Diatomaceous Earth (also known as DE, fossil flour, or fossilized phytoplankton powder)

How can I use it?

To kills bugs and internal parasites; for polishing, deodorizing, detoxification, and for general health.

Where do I find it?

Widely available through pet stores, garden centers, herbal suppliers, and online sellers.

What are the risks?

Generally regarded as safe for animals and humans. If taken internally, begin with minimal dose, and build up slowly.

FURTHER READING

Here are a few resources freely available on the internet, if you want to learn more.

Arizona Cooperative Extension. (2006). **Diatomaceous earth: A reduced risk pesticide.** Retrieved from http://ag.arizona.edu/urbanipm/pest_press/2006/september.pdf. Describes ways of applying DE as a pesticide.

Daniel, D. K., & Knight, G. D. (2009, April 2). **Mad as a hatter.** Retrieved from http://www.weston aprice.org/environmental-toxins/mad-as-a-hatter. Discusses DE as a cheap, safe, and effective agent for removing toxic metals from the body.

Earthworks Health And Solution Technologies, Inc. (2012) **Earthworks Health: Human Use Testimonials.** Retrieved from http://www.Earth workshealth.com/human-use-testimonials.php. Customer testimonials to health benefits of DE.

Hillier, R. (2009, April 23). **Food grade diatomaceous earth: kills parasites, bugs, and lowers cholesterol.** Retrieved from http://www. examiner.com/article/food-grade-diatomaceous-earth-kills-parasites-bugs-and-lowers-cholesterol.

Hope, B. (2011). **Diatomaceous earth.** Retrieved from http://www.deq.state.or.us/er/docs/Lower Bridge/ DiatomaceousEarthFactSheet.pdf. Discusses the safety of DE.

Quarles, W. (1992). **Diatomaceous earth for pest control.** *The IPM Practitioner*, XIV(5/6). Retrieved from http://www.freshwaterorganics.com/DE PestControl.pdf. Discusses DE as a non-toxic pesticide in gardening and livestock feed.

ABOUT THE AUTHOR

L. A. Nicholas, Ph. D., is a "naturalized Texan" who hailed originally from Alexandria, Louisiana, where she learned to love the outdoors and bug repellents. After completing too many years of higher education in the Midwest, she returned to North Texas and put down roots in the Dallas-Fort Worth area, where she eventually returned to graduate school to earn a doctorate in the literature of the Western cultural tradition from the University of Dallas.

Dr. Nicholas has lived and taught languages, literature, and humanities in several American states and two foreign countries. After a five year sojourn in southern Indiana, she now is planning to stay put in Texas, where she considers herself a "cultural missionary," writing for and teaching anyone who wants to learn the great treasures of the Western Cultural Tradition (currently under the auspices of the Walsingham Society of Christian Culture and Western Civilization).

She believes in lifelong learning, personal responsibility, and honest living, and has dedicated her life to the proposition that anyone who wishes to do so can learn to be smarter, live more fully, and grow wiser. Through her writing she hopes to help others do so.

CPSIA information can be obtained
at www.ICGtesting.com
Printed in the USA
LVHW011350080822
725426LV00009B/546